ISBN: 978-1-937658-99-1

Design and typesetting by Janet Evans-Scanlon
Text set in Garamond
Cover Art by Alice Hameau, commissioned by La Maison de la Poésie de Nantes and Mobilis
for a tour in the Pays de la Loire organized by the Collectif Lettres sur Loire et d'Ailleurs
Cover Design by Mary Austin Speaker

Cataloging-in-publication data is available from the Library of Congress

Nightboat Books
New York
www.nightboat.org

WHAT I KNEW

ELENI SIKELIANOS

NIGHTBOAT BOOKS
NEW YORK

[…]

In this house, everything is said.
The plastic animals are arranged in conference on the wooden stool near the toilet seat.
They have been curated to speak.

Speak.

[…]

Now I tell what I knew in Texas

Then I will tell what I knew in France

In Charleston we ate button candy near the sea

In Athens I heard that suck of shoe on pavement, in Arkansas my Greek
　　said, "I thought your Clinton was from Our Kansas"

Bossing pussy church bells in Connecticut and I knew how to spell it

I heard the phlegm-ridden ignition in Denver

When my birthday poet rubbed tree bark on his jaw saw I North Dakota

　　Sun befall me Idaho

　　Rainbow sleaze in Colorado

　　Sun befall me Michigan

Detroit's bus bearings squawking like a hurt-up parrot

We use human words in Indiana but not in Mississippi

Any babe comes out of a mother in Ohio, free state

Free-base in New Jersey and burn your face

Litanize the ills of Philly, Camden's demise

In the Wonder Masquerade of Florida saw I the black duct tape across the voter's thigh

Now I tell everything

I heard & knew

lightning

truth

war

earth

Somewhere someone has my hometown to himself

When I remember the tiniest leaf in California I cry, I can't
    afford it

Lord in my dream

a cheerful androgynous sexy woman leads me toward Seattle in the dawn

It's Claude McKay disappeared in Morocco in a storm and Mark McMorris thought
   to look for him from Spain

"If We Must Die" in Elaine, Arkansas, let it be a red red sky for everyone

Everybody saw it, say it

I shook the peach tree in Boulder, 5 peaches fell down

Blue is bisexual in Arizona but doesn't show it

Blue biseveral in San Antonio is what I call it and blue

    is to be words with me

Apocalypse's scavenger landscape moves through all the air

like a sandstorm in Oregon where I

Build my house of consciousness
Build my house of language-states from scrap
Build me clean, clean water

Soon, the water is not friendly, the hearts
are not soft, the setting is Alaskan with agitated waves and waste
In this landscape I am a stranger to myself
I am a friend to caribou
and the mines leach toxic

You can borrow my gloves in Colorado or call me Frankenstein, but you cannot
play kissy kissy in Bulgaria or a cold foreign city where the dark will fling you a
    stale cup/a *sale coup*/
a *dirty trick* once you've reached Toulouse

Now the scene is Athabascan, north, open, stark
Our boat is mashed by angry waves in the Chukchi Sea
One small girl (it could be you) clings to a shred of wood
The whales the waves are not wounds nor compounds they aid her therefore
do no wound to the waves or whales, people
an octopus can sing in his best Popeye voice
an otter can sing in her best fur-starry voice
a narwhale can brandish her tusk under the pack ice
like a drowned sailor corpse and a one-toothed unicorn

Human, who is your clade your cradle Pepsi
who is your species and all your descendants
A small human girl can cling to a wooden raft and make it to shore, make it to shore

Now how will we live on a human earth in a human sea

Now I will tell of a long low adobe
on a New Mexican land with poets speaking of drunks and politics and we
build a house from steel or steak or bricks
build the stars from steak or steel or bricks
build a cow from the bottom down with RNA interference
build a GM cow to give human milk in Hamilton
        Daisy's genes once told her to include beta-lactoglobulin
WAVE THE INTERFERENCE WAND
        Now she is born without a tail
        Daisy, Daisy in the daisy chain
        has never had a calf but can
        make milk for her human babies

In Honolulu we were asked to make likenesses more realistic than ourselves
Take a lump of gum or earth or clay
Make steak
Make human steak
Hold up the fascia   white sheath with holes   see the light through the meat

[…]

Cut the mold from the apple, and the core.
Gather the peaches and place them
on a yellow plate.
Smashed the fruit fly.
Ate the cold plum.
Opened the door.

[…]

In Toledo, acquire a Mexican boyfriend who desires a Spanish grant.
In Helena, kick a bale of hay down a slope, and I will catch it with my dim-thigh-light.
In Regina or in Boston, dream a prelude to the parachute of day.
Sealed for your protection in Old Bombay.

You are a visitor here.
The belly lifts up with the effort of the "b."
Because consciousness can tendril in any
direction in time

watch the self move away in the mirror

Watch it wolf away, World

World Human.

Be a Mammoth Carcass Found in Siberia
Turkey in New Syria Retaliation
Saudi Anger at Poultry Price Hike
Will Brown's brown face looking out from 1919 Omaha
on the white faces in this house.
In this house, we are asked to speak.

Requested to speak.
Required to speak.
The cat snores on the counter.
In this house, we master the facts
Swat the flies

The daughter is doing drills "if there's someone with a gun," and crouches
This is how she learns in school.

She is more toward the future (than me)
& will feel the past farther (away)

Everything on her face
Veers toward sunlight or tears
Around feeling like a wild

Groundhog arising to such and so late an hour so
Rest on my pale Natchitoches & sleep
Awhile, Daughter, caught in
Canary light or kindly
Earth with all your Extra light

and I will tell you of a time before Father
when Ft. Worth had yet to be Pasadena or Beeville Brownsville Tamaulipas

and the world accordioned out accordingly like a stairwell from dirt to sky

In Shreveport you will be tickled on the ankle by a bee
In Troy, bees will sow their own ipseity
      being only and always themselves, whether together
      or apart, bees sweeping equal spheres
      along perfect planes of intersection or
      overnighting in your cucurbit, mathematically precise
      before you even heard of hexagons or had eaten honey

In Pensacola or old Thebes you will admire and be admonished by a bee

And it follows that much of what we knew in Minden was known by others too

But I held a little freckled starlight in my hand, just for you

On a bus through the modern town of ancient Boeotia, the red poppies gathering
	round, see
gypsy camps in daylight and car exhaust encircling us

Now I tell like a bad body image in SoCal
how this impression of erogenous color draws a mask
right on the skin in Aden or
this B-named drive in Pensacola is mute like a road
is mute even as rain voices itself against asphalt

as Planes Bomb a Syrian Town Held by Rebels
and Florida's Officials Defend Different Racial and Ethnic Learning Goals
and in Pakistan they'll shoot a girl right in the head for going to school
and in Lebanon
and in France

sex marriage sex
same
right
to choose
if the subject is or was a human being, "who"
renewable(s)

How do you say Black shadow of a moon in Japan
How do you say Shadow, say Shadow of a tree in Malagasy

And when and why the sky looks blue in Argentina, scattered
by nitrogen and oxygen in Guiana

the hole above our heads widening each winter

and thus why the sky
and thus why

In this house my daughter asks me over dinner do you believe in god

                                            got

   fed up
with my hedging pseudo antihegemony
it would be upsetting if you were an amethyst she says let's stop
talking about it   are you   an atheist or an altruist
                   I'm a wannabe anarchist, pro-fantastic

then night transpired
a dark piece of moss
in a plastic bag
dragged across my forehead
      amethyst befall me Idaho
when dads were alive, bright-souled, shy

Just as
Once a
Neophyte

Prince came running across
Our faces / spaces
Understanding all
Ligatures between the two like sisters
In love with the same sea

and the Falklands were not an issue
and Western Sahara was peaceably shared
President Mohamed Abdelaziz Meets Irish Minister of Foreign Affairs
and who owns Badme, Bakassi, Banc du Geyser or Bir Tawil (no-man's land *de jure*)
Sahrawi
buffer zone
Bethlehem
referendum

Toni, you're a Texan
but Niwot's got you come nighttime
Come nighttime
I'm gonna come here, live here, and I'm gonna be better than before
before I was with you
bathed in starlight

in the dusty light of Cuisnahuat

Soaring Homicide Rate in U.S. Cities
Oil Rig's Owner Settles Gulf Spill Case
Malala Yousafzai's Parents Arrive at UK Hospital
Murder Charges Are Filed in New Delhi Gang Rape

And what I know anywhere
the world is a dangerous place for a girl
In Colorado or in Salt Lake City a girl splits herself in two
to protect herself in Swat

to tell if he's killed before
                    examine the crime scene
he knows how to dismember a girl near Ketner Lake

he's killed before
he's killed before
Don't write those words
Don't write those words

why take my emotion away (grey)

put it over there for now (Big Dipper)

catenary slide from sky to Kathmandu can always bring your feeling back

what protection for the girl-body, fluid-body, any body?

found a man-body under blankets in Flagstaff down by the creek
where the father's body was once kicking H
frozen, flowering at the chest
his heart was bumped   was hunched and hurt

Were you going to leave your father and let the wolves eat him?

Some bodies
can never be found and some
can never be bound

And in Seattle where it always sounds like someone's taking a shower
it smells like dumb luck
in muscular Seattle rooted down in its piney ground

the light is blind
& she is there

Susqually'absh
People of the Grass
        and a brown-haired boy, Highway 5, in the car next-door biting
                    into a Subway   vicing   innocent   speeding
      around Puget Sound

I want to know a small world away from Medicine Creek Treaty   rising Tumwater and
any river's watershed   plus
Large Americans anywhere
O large Americans, love of

Shoeless in Seattle stress
relief therapy   in the child's poem a potato
falls on the pop
star's head (it's Justin
Bieber's)

I will not
look this up
on the internet   why the blue
portion of white light
from the sun is
   scuzzily   scattered
over Rangoon and Kuching

All I know is blue

And in Colorado I will tell you

Crows in the snow   Hello.
Crows in the snow   Goodbye.

                                (*Hei-hei*, Anselm Hollo)

Also, a crane on the sky-
line glints from the high-
way ,　geese strip across the dinosaur
　cloud loping, skidding behind it
This is a world. This is a world-
view　/　Happiness every day in America

what we come to know and how we know it
and here I pile all I do or will not know

  "pony," "brake," "star," "oak," "green," "ridge," "tree," "to hide," "to flee"

How do you say Whenever they dance let me see near Sacramento?
The crackling blackbirds behind the words in Pipil?

I don't even know what I am.
Which brings me here.
        To the god of all my gemstones
              crackling potent violet flame St. Germaine

In the morning a man with glasses gets

into a car & I think It might be Kenneth Koch because I

am a poet and he is a poet. But this is not New York & Kenneth Koch

is dead.

The world is poor.

What is poverty?

Mother

I am a rich relation.

I am a poor friend.

Poverty is the bodies

gone into the ground making

the ground rich, she said.

One sack of rich rice   *For goodness sakes, Max,* the blonde

could do what   mother passing me said.

in the world.

The mind is awake in the twilight

a receptive wave

hovering

like a flying saucer in the dim light

a bowl of milk around which

the flies have gathered.

They are fireflies.

What I am I cannot say.

But will tell of all I heard and saw when I was in

an ancient world, holding

tablets of red rock

up to the sea-cave roof to show

we're ancient too, to fit time

back together   as if

you could reconstruct a broken brain and face

a human world and race

an animal symmetry lounging into the future

Max is apparently the dog.

in somewhat the same way a scarab beetle's blue

has no blue but coils in a peculiar

cellular

twist, like an onion's skin, and light

                              filters   down

through layers to give structural color, bouncing

back blue   .   That kind

of complexity.   (For kick, fur glow, I know a few other cells do

a few other colors too.)

Saw I radar pulses, freeways, Home Depot, Whole Foods so that everywhere
looked like everywhere else America, yet

Every late
Light returns to its own rewards
And finds itself early once again,
Young,
New,
Enlivened — so

sun befall me Sinai
sad in rainbow sleaze and
happy sparkle bunny Sarawak

and in Germany the wall had fallen so we collected bits of rubble

in Morocco the Arab Spring huddled at the hotel bar where I was asked not to speak
    against the king

or risk knowing disappearing too much

Alabama war unicorn ghetto nature Madonna in a cage

skeleton genes Eugene South Dakota Qatar there I go and know a thing but
    never pass a face that is my face

in Evansville North Dakota Fez Algiers Kandy and Carlsbad

The candidate was there with his billionaire saying

I will show you

      Divination by rats

      Which rat do you choose

      Stroke its fur

      Which rat do you choose now

      Rub its head

      This big rat tells me

      "You will move smooth through the world

      Your limbs will be oiled and elegant

            rolling softly in their sockets

      You will take a rattling bus to Lefkas

      in the honeymoon's ruin of Greece

      where the nation bifurcates

      between where you can get

          & what you can't"

Rat, rat, rat-a-tat

Soft-furred, shiny

Eat dandelion, sweet rat

[...]

Slept late like a rat.

[...]

How do you say Lovely star pawlight in the river in Oaxaca

How do you say A Mobius strip juggled on waves in the Java Sea

When men & women leap from crowned towers crumbling & I sit musing

on what our selves sound like

I think so, the river

makes sounds for the river

lead my blood

toward moonlight—

inevitably, flood—

[put thoughts in a china dish and ram them home]

rushing air without moving

In my ear I hear it writ in King I

drape clouds across our many faces (dark and light stars shining in dark sky, so

the faces of our people)

thus the ground of my experiment, I

what I

say & see

& think

to know or

don't I

don't

seem to have any way to see

what I

don't know and throw

the web over my head as if

it were a knowledge net but

still can't see the holes

          The men

are in the trees outside my window   I don't know why

they are "the" men or the window "my"   but I

see them   I see them saw

the tree

   "mud," "lake," "sky," "red," "sad," five," "to split," "to see" or "saw"

      will make a world if you swirl them

and Kansas is composed of corn and spinning jennys

To destroy exactitude through a small window in Moscow
Your tuna cans are confiscated getting onto a plane in Nairobi

And in Goma the mountain gorillas are at odds with rebels — anywhere
is dangerous to be a primate

antimeria yourself in Aurora
be a girl in Juárez   (please, keep her safe)

the sky is
threatened & threatening in Kampala   it's
                    death doing it
     in San Feliz

How best to represent an image of nothing in La Paz?

military action was suspended in Egypt
we demilitarized the verbs under oceans and overseas
the weight of information was too much in Oakland

In this house, the husband suspects he is surrounded

by anarchy. Four females in varying degrees of revolt.

The daughter eats pasta with her fists.

Elderly cats shit on the floor.

He suggests anarchy requires a witness

a system

to be outside

Now his daughter has just flicked some food on the floor.

Still, he is

Loving all the details

At a distance but

Igneously as if

Revved by silent engines up and

Down a

Hundred

Underground caverns where stars are

Nursed by lions or sirens and live

To tell the tale

And I too will tell all I knew and saw in Juba

shirtless women in straw skirts holding it together

tall Dinka men in blue robes smoking long pipes against the low horizon

Will our worlds live on?

In D.C. the former first lady is mothering and in charge, she gives me a bath and a book
with just-about-real clouds vibrating in blue on the cover

At the new president's house, the citizens are doll-sized, and have a good time
Knowing the lit bulb of each face on earth incandescent, ruining

The skies overbright with it

Outside L.A. highway rain makes each miling car a private dress for us

There's no dossier on it: in the dream we cross a metal bridge on mopeds, over oceans;
to the right: the snowy peaks of Scotland where we'll finger a blue
    scarf under an all-animal rain and
    feel refreshed from the sheer animalness of it

Near the Rockies, we get much older and learn Eternity is like
Infinity in time and teach it to our daughter

Metadata is out there

The bodies stacked in the morgue
The calcium livers of stars
That's what we do in the night.
Pass out.
Invent fake Googlemaps.

If we own the body or own up to the body
    in Praetoria
we'll congregate in meetspace, "a mute
    apostrophe flying through time"

Should I know   how to speak
Should I speak   how to know
      zodiacal light, airglow

in such brightening skies

      turn any epiphany around, when to me
             he appears like a god   from Sappho
I learn the verb: *phaino*
    "to appear" "to seem"
        as he sits talking to you
and against it she detonates a prefix: *epi*
    "on" "upon" (in space or time) "toward" "close" "near" "at" "among" "against"
    I manifest, I reveal
        hard by, "above" you,
           love, I appear: *epiphaino*

as Sappho did, like her own aphroditic epiphany, an unsearchable
bright stain spreading
through the holes of history

a sodium light heralding
what is utterable or un-
in our speaking, living
in our hypophanic, our undersleep, so

    see the lightning
    smell the truth
    hear the war
    touch the earth
    everybody say it

    lighting truth war earth

Ark is of my spirit   I'm telling the audience
    but they just keep talking
        toward the Unclaimed Zones of Outer Space

Make a Worldview
    and stand by it
Spot my
    blind
vision of the blind fact

After a night of tornadoes
Translate the term a gibbous moon moans in English

How can I get to Rethymnon, where the moon's face pulls
    silt from the sea floor, to swim
    in the nitrate-silver waters
    of πόθο ("desire," I remember on waking), Desire's
    silver waters rising with the moon.
We're in the religio-military citadel, concrete-grey and a flag
    fluttering in its heart — and we want to turn its waters back
    to Silver, Silvery
    Desire. In the guidebook, the Great Crater (a blasted dark
    moonscape, miles
    and miles of post-apocalyptic lizard and thick rock) is
    another place you can visit in the capito-human-desire landscape.

And at Naropa I'm trying to teach, students are reviewing our themes.
    "How to do things / make things," they say, and I say "This
    is how genesis is related to Time. Get rid of Time. I'm sick of it."
        But what do I mean?
    "How to make bread," someone says, and I want to say
    "How to jump out of a tree," but can't imagine
    how the instructions could be
    any longer than that You just
    do it You just
                jump

In the Mission my brother shows me
    cascading stylesheets & speaks
        of programmer yoginis
        all the color and size of a soldier

you see your arm floating above your head, skin in
    water, you're in an irrigation ditch in Afghanistan, the arm
        is no longer attached to its shoulder nor the word
           to its socket

Why wouldn't I believe these colors, like the fable that feels
more certain than reality which deforms in the speaker's mouth
each word she tries to make more real

just as
Zoic rock displays traces of life
Even to our stone-blind eyes, earth cracked open to what once was hiding,
Kissing deep time in
Each of its mineral outposts while

832F, alpha female of the Lamar Canyon pack
Is Killed Outside Yellowstone
Qatari Poet Mohammed al-Ajami Gets Life
("Jasmine Poem" A Threat to Emir)
Eyptian President Poised to Allow Civilian Arrests

another name, clearer than opinion, darker than knowledge

a victim of the loosened fact

and now I tell how on Aeroflot I saw the flight attendants with large hairs on their chins
who barked and served boiled Chernobyl meat and pressed Chernobyl cheese
in the white nights of Moscow the hotel guard with his rifle and the cleaning woman
    with her mop;
"America good," she said; "Russia good," I said; this was 1986

in any of my dreams there is a baby or a baby's head about to fall off a boat
or a baby placed on a bathroom shelf with no guardrail
which must be about the ditch of the future

in the present, on a train toward SeaTac I think How does a man with a big mustache
    eat much pussy
and then we're in a wedding or a war or
both at once, the ungulates mill about us, the cats and dogs have been abandoned
the flowers are richly colored but no longer perfumed

in this world

you will run through the grass and
you will walk down a hill and
you will come to a rock and you
will walk over a bridge and
you will get in a car and you will

come to a town of roundabouts
by the sea

that allow a mind to spin in rounding arcs like a silver coin whirling on a light-filled table
as the world's ripples —

                          — human, animal, parsec, political, paramecium —

— continue to ripple

how beautiful bad splash in Body
"1 corner   night shift"

in the museum in San Francisco I heard the small attendant say "My name is
    Apollonio Mission Control Chop, just ask them
at the front desk"
and saw the painting in which
the painter's toothbridge looked lunar, like a hand, her
    meaty, spiritual, punishing Rose hanging ever in my mind

in this house, my daughter's oral story begins:
    Once upon a time in the 1970s there was a guy going poo
    in a pot-chamber
but does not continue
(Currently, all her stories begin in the 1970s and end with shit)

In Madeira saw the magic length of god asleep under the table
U.S. Frequency allocations along the Radio Spectrum

"an 'I' without guarantees" foundered in Ft. Collins
passive space research lapping at its shores

I shifted this you toward me
and held it gently to my mind
like a blue flame
in a gone hand

Rain in the night.
Fog in the morning over hills.
Susie's heifer was impregnated too early by the bull.
Blue sky scratching through.

    "hood," "hound," "to hover," "to fly"
        turn left before the branch of these words to see the old cemetery

so singing sing I
    who is *not not an I*   (Bob Kaufman)
    I been to Walgreens
    I been to Walmart
    I crossed the ocean for a cheaper toy

Seen men in America in tight pants running across fields and looked away
American dishwashers sounding surely they are
    slaughtering someone

        sisters, mothers, fathers, daughters, brothers

Now I tell all I saw in California the fawn
    smashed in the road & dragged beneath the chassis like getting thumped in the heart
    but will tell
the circling hawk   the hovering kite   and must admit
basic things like I don't know how to see
    a billion   let alone
        S E V E N

    O bright terrestrial object
pollia condensata (in Zimbabwe), bluest
    berry ever to reflect light
            vs. darkest fabric ever to absorb it (the brightest is made by nature, the
    other, chemical, trademarked and — made by: man)

We saw themselves looking in at the window

in the Office of Spectrum Management
all our strong words were gathered

on a honey-colored bush
the words burning at the tips
of each / branch ,   being
burned / away —— all the good strong
offensive overly emotional French
words   There were words

being purged   on blackened bushes

on clear ones   Now how

will we say anything

strong without all our good strong words?

                              Fuck you. Says the words.

   Change the world. Say it.

     lightning truth war earth

in Denver saw I sweet Polyhymnia's stone ass hauled from the slopes of Vesuvius

and Pompei gladiator graffiti: CELADUS SUSPIRIUM PUELLARUM

                              ("Celadus makes the girls moan")

that night I dreamed a Japanese

or Uruguayan or

Italian poet

wrote the sound of a unicorn unwinding

silent in two instances

ζ

ξ

and sounded in the last

[sound here, if listening to recording]

each body gets to write their own

swirling

ideogram

to stand
for this lava ground grown richly black and into which
we one day dive head-first

Well, lake, rise up

        to show me all I know and all
                I can   — whoops —
                                    Nothing

    rattling in the knowing-tin

I will not rush to the internet to learn to say water
in Russian

water-flower-tree
hana-mizu-ki
(dogwood)

Then I knew the unicorn's horn unfurled to uncurl our own nations, shoulders and necks
That's called unwinding at the end of a long
Time

   ⁓

put on your military drone wardrobe

splatter it across the face

put on your soldierly attire before the raw war will end

what the wound you bind the world with

drape your asymmetrical thought around it, tight, soft, bright

what I saw in Suez: a barge & revelers thrust toward endocrine disruptors

thus I put on my PCB body burden, bathed in it

my polybrominated diphenyl ethers

my halogenated aromatic rings kissing the wet wrist round the sleeve

to put your lips where a fly has been

    "knowledge, the contaminant" (Williams, *Paterson*, p. 177)

to put your finger where PBDEs have been

    "knowledge, the contaminant" (Williams, *Paterson*, p. 177)

to wake up with Derrida on your face

do you have any friends

any human dog friend I say

        to the tall white girl, to the queer Black man in my dream You are invited

to a reading group sleepover at my house

we'll scrape for scraps of food

we'll eat scraps of sleep

    "By now we are tired of being amazed" (Levi, *If This Is a Man*)

Waterfall allow us
laughing in a new key now
God's plan Happiness:

to see a beaver in the rivers of New Jersey, near the Newark
airport like
seeing a brown
furry jewel   rectangle of
sun
reflected in the eye, my
eye (brown), which I can't see but see
a thin wet log with a tail arrowing
across — it's not even a river, it's a ditch, & it seems to take forever
to get a small way, like a ship on the horizon compared to a bee
between two poppies (Proust), also (revision)
it's possibly a
muskrat, can't
see
the tail & caught it
from the corner
of my eye, eye
to tail, tail to eye, creature
to creature, jewel to jewel, beaver
to muskrat, river to ditch, world
to world we
live here and who here

reads me as

theirs? I mean what group

of humans

come

get me the woman

with a phone to her head

says   This is all taking place

on a train in a station text

your name

to this world   I am suddenly

in love

not

with this world but

with New Jersey, the old

country, where I can know on the internet later

"beavers on the rise in NJ" (don't even have to talk to anyone)

Internet cat stars scratch the surface of time

And time is the material poetry is and is not

This poem is antigrowth and has no needs while

Alawite Demonstrators Clash with Police

New Generation of Defectors Expose North Korean Abuses

Obama Nominee Behind 'Driving While Black' Case

Stopped for gas in white Nixon's hometown

Dreamt the bathroom heaters of SoCal kept me warm & kept me down

Everything in California but Bakersfield & Reagan made sense to me

I knew which knobs to turn on the stove in strange houses without looking

If a machine were to become an animal not

the other way

around I would know it in Knowlton where the mayor says "Our Beavers

Are Criminal Geniuses"

beavers never do bad karaoke by Björk

beavers like us are captives/spy-heroes trying

    to overthrow the cruel and tall Overlord, docked

at a distant port; our crime: being women and beavers, or poor and poets or black and

    human, luckily

centaurs are on our side   we are

enveloped in a bubble of electric light and trying

to save the world

from ourselves

now nowhere near Normandy we are eating our way out of cages

a souk of metal coops stacked in the will's wild array

& I who am also you must chew through whipped cream and wire

to escape the pursuers / as prey

In Cuba, at Camp X-Ray, don't let your chewing jaws give out, give way

In this housE, my daughter's Voice peeled A slice
of consciousness off sleep like
a slice of flesh I no longer needed

so I reconcile myself to time and time's
so-it-was, although

in an unnamed place near Yuma you can take a backward train to the Tower of Youth
    which is more like a waterfall or a sheet of glass stacked by the tracks
where youth is
the you-were just as

the young men went into prison & came out old

it will not all come out in the wash

        lightning   truth   war   earth

their young youth squeaking inside their old bones

Now Portland's sort of in the picture and we're slogging through night, town-by-
    town, tooth-by-tooth
to get to all potential before it's scraped to the stripped bone
like all that could happen in the world but doesn't crammed in one bus
and sent home

Aced the mountain in the dark, soaked thru & thru
without knowing what mountain is made of nor the answer in the morning of the
    visual henceforth yet I kiss you in the evening near the corner bar exclaiming

If lace were lazy & face were facing
you

I say the you lightly as if
pressing my fingers
to your cheeks
I'm driving which makes it
dangerous & more
intimate

Meteor Shatters One Million Square Feet of Glass in Chelyabinsk

And in my brother's mother's house in Santa Barbara my brother is explaining
    waterboarding
to my daughter
"It's like if I wrapped a wet towel around your head and poured water on you and…"
this is to explain the word "inquisitor" in *Harry Potter*
"Wait, what?" she says. He describes it
again: "Like if I was trying to get information out of you and I…" "But you
would never do that

to me," says she.
"Probably not," his reply.

Jingle-jangle, my mind's a tangle
Overhung with what we've undone. Please put *grace* back in
Scapegrace for my brothers to hold close to all
Elegance and I will celebrate a
Funus imaginarium — funeral rite for my

unnecessary selves, all of them, built publicly

Does a nation regard its selves as such or the ones it wants to show and allow us
    "to censure" "to pillory" "to savage or rush or blitz"
piss those into a pot, pour out, replace with

what does a moon jelly (medusa) think about
all day

The House of Our Undoing
The House of Blood Mysteries
House of Lost Contexts
The House of Pretexts
House of the Snake-Knot Starting at the Gut and
    Stolen Elections
Seeing with No Brain to Say What You Saw

I want to think about that
barn full of doors with poets' names on them
enter each one for succor
for Caroling Dawn, Cooling Down, for a Context Disassembled Come Dark

Awake, I found

a blackberry stain on my constant daughter's pink mermaid
pillow, tracked over it by my leather slipper. If it were you.
Crushed drupe.

I dreamt the world
without the world
what I mean by that
is
not our blue blackberry-like globe seen spinning
from the dark sky
but the bruisy sky spreading out in every direction, unending and without
p.o.v., pricked
with lace of

light — and

no shape to it—
not the shapes we know, anyway—
also

when I woke up I thought I forgot what the world was like
without the internet, which means I remember what it was like
though I can't explain it —
for the first time,

C.D. Wright is dead today.

I was born
I don't keep on doing it
but I never stop having been born
even when I'm dead
I'm going to claim that space

Chatoyant Descent
Constellated Dervishing
Cimmerian Descant
Chickweed Dear
C.D.
Chromospheric Duende
Chronologically Detasseled
There you are —

a mystery note that adheres to the ear beyond understanding fluttering in a dark wind
or cells that grow with the mice (glia) gleefully and the night — .

Left the parking
spot. and left the parking
lot. Poets
will never stop
looking for the rock
at rock bottom

in the task
section of my phone
I will hymn him and her and them—
our God's tall shingled windmill

In the Cleveland airport (my grandmother once gigged here) I look around for some remnant
of burlesque
find it
in the man playing iPad solitaire and the American Kill List
shrinks and grows in the night like a wind unsyllabled toward Cincinnati

to be in love with that rough wind
or on a road trip near strong water
which comes rushing up sea — roiling, muscular, glauque, cold, mucusy — to be
a powerful roving liquid eye flecked
with white spittle — to be
a whole dream screen filled with fresh sea, sea that will
always outlive you/me

oh my hallucination's hyacinth
saw I the white fathers and sons of Geneva, NY, red-cheeked, fleshy, near white
    houses which I mistake for the lake
critchiticrotch I pitch the clock
into the lake scolding bad
Jack Spicer stuck in the trailer
home of death
you, you, I sputter between gritted teeth
Jack Spicer's face flickers out of screen
You have taken the bread when others were hungry
You have left my friends and favorite poets out of the anthology
I enter [god's] trailer to take back a bit of baguette
but find a cigarette

can't smoke it, since I quit

So sun befall me Baltimore
Rainbow sleaze Guantanamo
Radiant thaw in Chicago
unsaying
if god is a mood
or god is

In this house
"I'm gonna step on bacon."
    —Eva, age 7, 12:46pm, Thursday, March 28, 2013, standing on the counter
"Seriously!" she says when I say I'm writing that down.

Make me
a heart that burns like Ephesus
a head that moves toward Rome
a heart that moves to the right (wrong) side of the body when

U.N. asks for $5 Billion for Syria
President O. Calls Surveillance Programs Legal and Limited
Rape and Murder Provokes Fury in South Africa
For Puerto Ricans, a Parade of Doubts
Officials Seek to End Protection of Wolves

in Siberia the cannon sounded — war
wrote Blaise Cendrars, who looked old as soon as he was born and
sounded like a teen until he died

and on Hydra where my Greek comes back to me I figure the plural of euro (euró)
and differences between the dirt below Juneau, Tallahasee, Annapolis and memory

in Yokohama we decorate the beach with our own shapes
which look like circles and municipalities, cargo ships and plates of giant sandy peas
we decorate ourselves in Tanaka's Electric Dress until we are
"High, trembling, swaying, low, sometimes leaning on the strong wind . . . until
    at least one of [us] flew away and never returned" (Jiro Yoshihara)

like Guillaume Apollinaire, though his lovebook did,

hidden in an artillery compartment for personal effects which I saw in the museum

    where a card said it was an object "intimate, combative, lyrical and public"

"Publisher: the artist, with the assistance of Sergeants Bodard and Berthier"

on the front, France, where 2 million died

(what image of it

could we

call to mind? of the world's X

million refugees?)

"It snarls the translucence" (Rachel Blau DuPlessis)

in Lyons, CO, my friend describes the bitch giving birth, a tan

German shepherd and three humans in the whelping room

on laptops looking up instructions on birthing canines not trusting

does a dog know

    "shop," "meat," "grief," "to glean," "to glow"

saw I on a train from Providence to Boston Greif Brothers Moving Vans

and climbed the tower-like chair C. & F.'s son made to look back at the moon

small moon

tall chair

spring peepers throwing voice pieces through air

mother says us in my mouth

hauls us up unbespoke to   be spoken

                              woken &

                              shaken

in lace light

meat-like

what does a murdered body

smell like?

like the Quaboag River   (question mark)

wandered I Mt. Auburn Cemetery where I ask Fanny about the afterlife

she says, I think it's happening all around us, folk-Catholics call it The Thinning

Is it a lake or a river?

Let's say it's a lake,

like The Oxbow

near Northhampton (Connecticut River)

or Songhua River, China [see picture]

Nowitna River, Alaska

"Swirls and curves, showing paths the river once took, as well as oxbow lakes, are

    easily seen

in this satellite photo."

The meander goes curved

The neck of the meander gets cut

Tourniqueted by time's flood

Take this abandoned meander loop
and hoop it round our human necks

you too are subject to hydraulic action, abrasion, corrosion
    hail, heat, drought, sleet, thunder

                lightning   truth   war   earth

torrent it
with love, and

    "If the weather's good we can go for a walk"

however we do   the future
the rain & the wind & the heat will happen, her un-
gentle blanket, I say <u>her</u> because I'm putting <u>her</u> in power for the future
feral weather Let her command it; crack
         it   καλόs
open with her hands
              good-human
crowd-sourcing the clouds across
the plains

parasite the light (cities)

learn how to gather

       "to sun" "to sweat" "to the dogs" "to eat" "to hunger"

Oh, right, I was one of those poor

kids in dusty shoes in love a few

lifetimes ago and discovered love

can control no weather or web but can

make the syntax go shaky

at its columns, like rosary hogans, trotting

amourous dogs across the big loco shining night and break it

open

as open

as weather

    ~

At night, the trees touched the ground and made places light wouldn't touch. And in the dark a child could be swallowed and her bones left for morning to find. There were fires and broken bottles and feathers, laboring day, and laboring night. The small prisons of boarded up discotheques and sweets shops. And from real prisons, the disappeared did not reappear. Down the street, a dead house. What's a dead house? It's not in ruins, it's dead, no plants grow there. It's a skull at the gates with a message: This could happen to you too.

crack in the flowered coffee cup, breakfast, bright kitchen, suburbs of Casablanca, do I heat the milk in it? Grates on the window, white towel on the line, shadow of clothesline on white wall

the flowering of detail, infinite

where we are sheltered from the search
or laid open

bud-tips from the silver maple (*Acer saccharinum*) damp
on the path (blue front door) (Colorado)

Eva-daughter at the grey table spooning rice from a white take-out container into
her green bowl (Colorado)

       the reactor

       Nuclear

       Heart atom

       o come

in Haifa I extract cold fact from the fictional archive
in Jaffa, the filmmaker splices his uncle back
to the old neighborhood (the one that no longer exists)
now his uncle can walk streets on screen as if

they'd never been shelled

some people find the trashed magnificent
trashed world
(you can do that if you get to choose
where to live in it)

Saw I at the Parc de la ligue arabe a pile of chicken heads outside the running track
& a German shepherd nosing over them, whining, hungry, tied
to the oldest gymnasium in Africa

We enter the oldest gymnasium in Africa (the limping guardian lets us in)—
ruined high art deco structure smelling of shit, pigeons, and damp stucco

Saïd Aouita trained on the track outside and broke 5000 and 1500m world records
Maryam and Sousen pull their scarves over their noses
no photos allowed
    of the feces, broken bottles, discarded pants
the guardian, Lancen Bilane, leads us upstairs
he was the hurdling champion of Africa in the 1980s, you will not
as of now
find him
with your search engines

all the other old champions arrive, a woman in hijab with a bad back, a man who
taught gym in Dallas before coming home

In the internet pictures, the park looks clean & beautiful.
In the park, the park looks dirty and ragged.
Where does the King live?
In Rabat and on in the mind where we are not allowed to take photos of the still
rides and dead birds in the closed-down Yasmina Amusement Park which Zineib
remembered from childhood.

Here is how we propose to change the Park:
Tie a piece of twine from trunk to trunk
Put a chicken head in the middle of the path
Put an orange rind in the middle of the path; record the ants
Pay 20 people 80 dirham a day to pick up the trash (can the King afford it?)

Record all the stories of the athletes at the track
Let the lady runner's back be unbroken, the gymnasium restored

What has changed the world more
Anger?
or Love? Yes
or No? When you know

please don't text but
whisper the answer most intimately to me
like a bit of dandelion tissue you've
susurrated toward my ear.

Now we are hiding in the Cupola together writing poems
We go outside to change a little something,
a mircobend in the frequencies.
As soon as I walk out I realize everybody's already changing something,
everybody's doing a bit of land art, cutting across the paths, arm in arm. Human
bodies moving against and over the curves of earth. Isn't that the solution and the
problem? I find a piece of glass leaning against a ficus tree, nestled in a patch of
grass. I move the glass. I move the grass when I move the glass. Change your life,
says Rilke, there is no place

Then there is the wind, it blows the paper threshold to the miniature tree house
the girls have made
away

That does not see you, he says

You must

*

in public space I polish my words I publish them
in their cacophony, a movement
of speech from outside to in, inside to out

& hope

*

for deepest encryption, dream in
cipher mood
that what's hidden or sheltered inside the who
can still be hid
that's what's
our private reserves
keep them
sparkly &
gold

*

saw I the eye of money in new Cancun and old New York

where any baby's old enough for money

"That kid's already the age of money," I heard in Brooklyn where I grew sick of money
    and money-color

in Benslimane I changed money for the perfect lover

the perfect lover is a clover

is the perfect lover over

the hills & over the dales

you will come to Jacksonville with a toothache and a limp

and you will get to Albany as soon as you've done the paperwork

where your new lover will steal your other lover's ring and lie about it

and the bus will bring you to Edgewater softly, wetly scratching up to ocean

but do not stop in Titusville where the Ais where wiped out by "slave trade, disease
    and rum"

In this house I fell asleep in my daughter's bed and dreamt they lit kindling under my
    feet (I must have needed to run)

while my daughter dreamt of a horse who ate rocks

and every time he ate a rock he grew another head

What color was he?

kind of champagne-colored

and every time he ate grass he grew another leg

but not necessarily another hoof

and every time he ate hay

he grew another hoof
and he was immortal
and every time he grew a leg
he lost one
He was self-sufficient, I'd say

And then we're walking north along the coast road above the roughened water
This means everything to me
to be so lucky to drive a Lexus through private groves near the sea, to be a techie type
    with perfectly organized shelving and always on my phone
pretending to be your bro while performing unsubtle acts of mind control
so every time you go online to find the translation of
    un visage, livide, terreux, ravagé   (Mohamed Leftah)
there appears a Unicode vision of fancy shoes AS IF
your dream mind had made them

        Will you let this Web know more about you
           than you yourself know?

at the end of the road the gorgeous ocean belongs to no one even if the clumsy hands
    of commerce claim it and

Court Rules Human Genes May Not Be Patented

saw I near les Habbous hillocks of old clothes and women sitting in the midst of them
piles of herbs & hanging jackal skins

in the Marché des Sorcières hedgehogs stuffed in wooden cages (one dead, another
eating its entrails), turtles, and a falcon awaiting event
henna stalls (by day) turned brothel shacks by night
where is all this seeing getting me?

an emerald invisible eye grows above my eyes
on the freeway outside the slums "if you've seen one sky you've seen them all," says
husband knowingly
yet all these skies begin to compile a kind of being we live within/beside

pony of regret
my sunglasses scratched in the rich man's house
we are travelers passing through this sprawling outpost, scratching back
but who are we, and where are we going, and how will we share?
somewhere of simplicity, contained in a single word in a woody room
that holds a poem
before time caught us in its sculptural fluidity
the CIA so secret to us then
each dark sheet of reality revealed as we peel back truth year by year
or down in the bosque among the scraps of toilet paper and dry pine needles
lying dying down

we have changed the limits of knowledge
if we think we have, have we?

   "to milk" "to blacken" "to blue"

"we know trailers" says the
mudflap, small
claim in a big
world, what
do you know?

we got here on a single-engine jet
our shadow moving against the shadow of the mountains, where the shadows fringe
over the tiny horses & houses
over the pock-marked fields
the computer knows where to put us down
what we ourselves don't know but hear
the muffled thunk when we alight next to the warehouses
where butterflies brought from Malaysia await their pavilions
and orb weaving spiders palp-type-tap against cardboard boxes, soon
to be trucked
to the realms of Natural History
ferrets sent from Cincinnati breeders are unboxed at the airport FedEx
and queen bee larvae anticipate their apiculturists

to speak in the tongues of angels and men
women and ferrets and djinns

In this house I write I hope all is well
at email's end — Hope all is well
in the world

where this poem

takes place

    in the tongue

        that talks in the night

in the limits of knowledge

    the knob of the palate

the palace of language where I walk clothed

palace of world, walk naked

to put the words together

    "violet" "violent" "eye" "to try"

to come right

   ~

In this house, we try to speak the words of it

The disasters touching each of us

tapping lightly at our temples with cool catastrophe fingers

daughter says she'll have a garage sale

"so when planet earth is dead we can fix things grow things again like compost we'll
   show them how to make compost"

where's our train going? asks the truck driver in Cipleyville, the town famed for its
   dream onions where radishes come alive in the night like ballet folklorico dancers

I'll take this train straight through the dusty light-filled tunnel peopled with dust-covered
   workers clutching our rakes and shovels; are we all going the same way?

We are.

Toward and among the years, traveling, unraveling.

In Antananarivo in an earlier era we learn there is little difference between an
   exploring ship and a slaving ship

These guns are haunted with history and will come to no good

Moving along wide rivers like robber-ghosts, and the glow-eyed lemurs in tangles of trees

What, I say, do these species have to tell me?

all animal and plant movement makes the earth's sounded score

"each body also becomes the tone of the text," said Anne, and I listened

                                   for she

                      is like

An antelope and a leopard at once, blazing in the same
Nerve-fire-synapse, all
Nets bound up
In
Eternity

I close my eyes, my lips, await snake communication
An elderly snake with ochre eyes moves toward me, up the back of my head, down
    my forehead, over my eyes to show me

darkness is also active
in its present and past

In this house: talkative hyped-up wall fly way past midnight

Love won't save it

but soon we'll find "a field where we bed down with what we love" (Duncan via Anne)

there is no way to say death exists, I said
First I said it wrong then I said it right
there is no way to say death exists

The chasm board trembled and all the objects on it
trembled   china thimble
rubber ball
all our details, belongings   all our us   in the earthquake of world

wanted to hold the kitten but the kitchen did not want to be held
wanted to hold life but light did not want to be held [felled]

because

a tiny winged bug of the most perfect spring green
landed on my book (drawn to the small circle of light) I put the book on the nightstand
a few pages later I scratch my outer forearm (a tickle) and there was the spring bug, ruined
Can I put it right?

In my dream, I figured out how to do the most perfect something but now
can't remember Was it
wash a muddy cow?
wail as long as requested in Sichuan?
cure a father-in-law crazy
with money? Deaf with money.
Save the spring bug?
Make a life into instant archive? In the
                              over-plenty of life

Campus Killings Set off Anguished Conversation About the Treatment of Women
276 Abducted Girls Still Missing

"everything" "made the same"
 "Who at this point 'knows' anything, reading so much?"

saw I in the Zone Experimentale near the banlieue starhope & fledgling lights
peaches picked yet still at work, alive, increasing their sugars
they inhabit a space "both crystalline and collapsible"

Stay here with me till the last hole of blue closes
(clouds cunt over air)
(the sky a snatch giving birth)

"I'm gonna go back into those bushes and get drunk" (grubby-fingered, trash-talking
    fishing bum)
Hey what time is it?
2:42 I yell back to another bum in the underpass on the rocks by the creek
2:22?
2:42 I yell then wonder if that precision will be useful
b/c my father was a bum I feel a daughter and even a mother to some bums
tho I myself have never been a bum strict sense
what is a bum strictly speaking?

bonus boners for all big billionaires
Eekonomics is how I feel about it

"Poetry with synonyms are beautiful use texting for it"

"my rhyming algorithms are going through maintenance synonyms are currently
   down Please come back soon"

outside Denver dusty green fields of broccoli near the airport & worker shacks
   shimmer under heat's calm hand
when I say "worker" what do you see?

"The calculated production of uncertainty"

Show me a river
Know me a word
Sixty-five   is the word
I heard lying beside you
When we lay
Down dreaming
Head-to-head
Love-by-love
Hard by the river

⌒

The last line of the uncorruptible poem is more beautiful & actually spells

Victory

Victory

⌒

In Boulder on 36 saw I the Buffalo Highway, but
only Broncos, Passats passed there
then I saw it all stripped clean
cars growing wooly back toward buffalos
all the metal & asphalt tipped & sliding right off the horizon, hooves stampeding

Mothertongue you're gonna come
into the fold
of what's
been done and make this
right

riding my bike with a flat tire down the wrong city streets

"On one hand, I feel knowledge as an air,
a sound the mind makes when it makes it" (Simone White)

on the other I
sang the song wrong then could only hear it erroneously:
LMNOP, Let it be
The yoga teacher says Feel your body sinking into the earth but we are on the second
    story

Below us is a bank
Feel your body falling through the floor & landing on vaults
Where we can redistribute the wealth
held in each muscle
like little wicks that forgot to reflame
human space

This is not a night of sleep
It's a house with the weight of the sleeper's vigilance
In this house, we wait
for "a bit of something *incognito* [to cross] over from night to day
[to] change the life of the sleeper" (Anne Carson)

Now in the morning Moms says mother-body stuff like
    Oh, my arm my back

In the mysterious concatenation of time that will soon be me

In the dream Selah says Mercury as if Mercury was her double, a female meme is a
    feme so

Take a picture of it and post. Oh, you can't, it's
my dream. (Big white rock face with flecks of gold.)

the most beautiful
gutter glut   in all sleepdom, a

g   ghost

ing   you can

     telepathy

         the senses afterward

              to me —

I.

I, future it.

I future it.

Sea, over there. (Points with all her fingers.)

See knowing in a silence between the bone & the skin in

wet psyche

dry words   the world

begins with a rupture

am I dumb enough

I think

money

yes

I am dumb enough

to write , to speak

dry mind

wet feet

cold stones, feet in the river

head in the clouds —— on the plane

I learn lenticulars

are moved by wind

lightning   truth   war   earth

singing & pointing

I begin   the world begins

without a right order of knowing

those who know and those who don't

emancipate, live

something for which you

were not born

A Note

At first, I wanted to keep the references in this book secret, because poetry is a secret way of knowing. A book of poetry is its own private knowledge house and a large share of the pleasure is the poet inviting you into their poem-room for a private, intimate séance, where just the two of you (you and the poem, with the poet as a ghost hovering outside the room) make meaning. I hope it's obvious that part of what I'm meditating on in this book is poetry's private, ancient knowing, older and stronger (if we remember it) than any stupid search engine.

I wrote this poem in 2013, before the revelations that Cambridge Analytica and other "friendly" ghosts (a different type of ghosts than poetry ghosts) were in fact running or trying to run large parts of our lives. If I'd written it last year or this, it would have been much angrier, but I hope still spiked with iron, humor, lift. The headlines are taken more-or-less verbatim from The *New York Times* in the months I was writing, and act as a kind of threshold between the interior knowledge of the poem and the spaces it might have to move across. Someone has called the brain the last private territory, but we now know that's a myth, too. Poetry may not be the total antidote, but it is a little spell to ward off the dark.

So, I didn't want to point out that each of my family members' names is embedded in this book as a gesture toward poetry-cryptography. Or that poems can indicate another kind of global network. Or to include a glossary of poets invoked, because poems have always named their familiars in a gesture toward not exclusion but inclusion: you can know my people, my poets, too. I would say it's a way of knowing that can't be sold back to us. We must keep our minds, our imaginations, resilient, bouncy. Don't let them sell us our private territories. They already belong to us.

Acknowledgments

Portions of this poem appeared in *Big Big Wednesday*, *Seedings*, *Second Stutter*, and *Fence*. Thank you to Molly Schaeffer, Jerrold Shiroma, Solomon Rino, and Rebecca Wolf, editors extraordinaire. Un grand merci à La Maison de la Poésie de Nantes and Mobilis, who commissioned the cover art for a residency/tour in the Pays de la Loire, and to Alice Hameau, who made it. The excerpt at the end of this page is by Jacques Roubaud, and is translated by Matthew B. Smith.

Thank you also to my dear ones who read the manuscript and offered advice and encouragement: Julie Carr, Brenda Coultas, Laird Hunt, and Doña Anne Waldman. Love you. Thanks, always, to Susie and Brown Bag Farms, person and place who/ that keep helping me write books. Thanks to MASNAÂ / L'Ecole for community in Morocco, France, and beyond. Eva, thanks for saying "I'm gonna step on bacon," and for calling atheists amethysts. I know that was a long time ago.

Historians will note that C.D. Wright died in 2016. The section in homage to her wrote itself in repeated shout-outs of her initials (crushed drupe, Cimmerian Descant, etc.), and demanded to be in company with the other acrostics in the poem.

I dedicate this book to my teachers.

   Truth enlisted   in memory's dance
     resists   in my voice   any manner
of reaching   the realm of
knowledge

ELENI SIKELIANOS grew up in California, and has lived in New York, Paris, Athens, Colorado, and now Providence, RI. When she was 20 years old, she left the U.S. and traveled for over a year, most often hitchhiking and sleeping outdoors, from London to Istanbul, Haifa to Cairo, Cairo to Dar es Salaam, Athens to Paris, where she settled for another year to work, read, study, and write. She is the author of eight books of poetry, most recently *Make Yourself Happy*.

NIGHTBOAT BOOKS

Nightboat Books, a nonprofit organization, seeks to develop audiences for writers whose work resists convention and transcends boundaries. We publish books rich with poignancy, intelligence, and risk. Please visit nightboat.org to learn about our titles and how you can support our future publications.

The following individuals have supported the publication of this book. We thank them for their generosity and commitment to the mission of Nightboat Books:

Kazim Ali
Anonymous
Jean C. Ballantyne
Photios Giovanis
Amanda Greenberger
Anne Marie Macari
Elizabeth Motika
Benjamin Taylor
Jerrie Whitfield & Richard Motika